Out of My
Mind

Book Four

Even More Late Night Contemplations
About Trauma and Neglect

By Ruth Cohn, MFT

To all the Blog Readers who told me that my weekly musings mattered to them.

And to my dear friend Dawn who said "these should be a book!"

Sign up to Ruth's email list to receive a free digital copy of *Cycles of Escalation*. A brief eBook which explores how to manage triggers within relationships.

www.ruthcohnmft.com

Contents

01 ——————

Sex Positive:

Climate Change,"Drudgery and Begrudgery,"Magnificence

Anyone who has known me more than a minute has heard me (probably ad nauseum) reference the renowned relationship researcher John Gottman. Gottman, originally an MIT-trained mathematician, changed direction to study psychology, mostly to try and figure out why he couldn't get a date. The result was 40 years of longitudinal data about what makes relationships work and the predictive factors of separation and divorce. He also wound up with his long-term partner and collaborator, Julie Gottman.

I have great respect, admiration, and gratitude for good researchers. I certainly would not be able to do it, and probably wouldn't care to, but research changes history and makes our work credible on a larger scale. It can also serve as an often much-needed guide, especially in psychotherapy, which hovers somewhere between science, art, and some think, alchemy.

One of my favorite tenets of Gottman's research is central to my work. It is the simple and undeniably well-proven principle that in a relationship, to break even –to simply maintain equilibrium – the ratio of positive to negative is (drum roll) 5:1. Just to break even. That means appreciation, compliments, smiles, and gestures of affection. It can be most anything positive to the other, measured against complaints, criticism, grumbles, and other negative interactions.

In the neglect experience, these random shots of positivity are glaringly absent. Our best hope may be to exist, which may not be such a positive thing. This is why I am always looking to inject positivity whenever I can, which is not always easy in the bleak landscape of trauma and neglect. As we know from operant conditioning, the principle on which neurofeedback is based, the brain responds most favorably and learns from reward, so positive feedback is, by nature, reinforcing. An additional win! 5:1 or better is a quick and sure way to change the weather in a relationship. Consider it a positive spin on climate change!

Gottman also reminds us, perhaps reassuringly, that evolutionarily speaking, relationships are significantly different now. It was not that long ago, in our historical past, that our species did not live long past our reproductive years. Once the mandate to preserve the species was accomplished, monogamous partnership was not, at least biologically, essential anymore. Now we live decades beyond childbearing and are challenged to maintain harmony, let alone eroticism, until death do us part. We are in a slow and trying process of changing nature's design.

In the neglect household, as in much of the world, sex is not talked about, and certainly not in any kind of constructive or instructive way. In the world of trauma, and in general, we mostly hear or speak about sex in its worst light: abuse, exploitation, trafficking, harassment, commodification, and aggression, both micro and macro.

I thought, how about ringing in this new year with something positive about sex? Next week is Chinese New Year, the Year of the Rabbit. A lover of animals, I appreciate the tradition of each year correlating to one or another species. Besides their reputation for liberally proliferating, I also like the idea of jumping, rabbit-like, into this year.

Drudgery and Begrudgery?

Sex-positive has become something of a buzzy designation, kind of like trauma-informed: a sub-credential attempting to offer a space safe where people are free to speak or be open about sexual matters and to be accepted and understood. When I first started training for sex therapy, I quickly discovered the work of Peggy Kleinplatz, whom I think of as the best sex therapist in the world. In addition, Kleinplatz is a researcher and a professor – truly a pro. When I first saw her at a conference, I was amazed at how such a giant could be so diminutive, with beautiful hair almost as long as she is tall. I hope it is not sexist that I describe her appearance, as I certainly do not mean to diminish any of her other attributes!

At one of those first conferences was an opportunity for "Breakfast with the Presenters." I managed to be early enough to score a seat at the smallish round table with Peggy Kleinplatz! I was so starstruck I really could not speak or ask my questions, let alone eat! We have since become friends, and I have since been the presenter at one of those tables. It is a distant and sweet memory.

One of Peggy's great achievements and contributions is that for several decades she has been seriously studying the positive: the elements of long-term, satisfying, monogamous sex. She has interviewed thousands of self-identified sexually happy long-term couples of every stripe to answer the question, how do they do it? How do they keep sex from devolving into "drudgery and begrudgery?" (Confession: I stole that catchy turn of phrase from Bono's recent memoir. The book isn't great, but that line is brilliant! I wish I could claim it!) Peggy came up with thousands of couples who could do it. (She studied non-monogamous couples as well, not to discriminate!) I was delighted when in 2020 she came out with a popular book, *Magnificent Sex: Lessons from Extraordinary Lovers*. Circumstances change, bodies change, and health intrudes, and yet these couples continue passionately going strong. How do they do it?

Magnificence

Everyone should read this book. I won't spoil it; I will
simply recount a few highlights. Peggy describes her
incipient interest in the project, which proceeded to
span decades. As I have said before, therapists, or people
in general really, enter the sex therapy field out of some
particular fascination (preoccupation?) with sex. It was
true for me. However, I was also faced with couples with
one or another iteration of a sexual impasse daily. Not
just sexual trauma, but trauma in general, including
neglect, can wreak all sorts of havoc in the sexual body
of an individual. Requiring a delicate balance between
sympathetic (excitement) and parasympathetic (calm),
the dysregulated traumatized organism is challenged.

(There is much more to be said about this expansive subject in future writings.) In the case of neglect trauma, abundant anecdotal observation has revealed complex sexual difficulties based on the profound ambivalence, if not crisis, about interpersonal need. The child of neglect is compelled by both interpersonal longings and terror, which creates an additional dilemma around sex.

Peggy began her exploration by asking new sex therapy clients who came in complaining of (or were being complained of showing) diminished sexual desire to describe their time of greatest sexual longing, realized or not. Remarkably, they all had some. Peggy says, if we want to inspire sexual desire, we must have a vision or experience of "sex worth wanting!" Seems so obvious, no?

I will jump ahead to the "lessons," partly because I encourage you to get it straight from Peggy (and her co-author, whom I do not know, but do not wish to neglect, A. Dana Menard,) and because I want to leave you with something positive. And admittedly because I risk going on all day about this!

The top three ingredients of magnificent sex, according to Kleinplatz and Menard's research, are (drum roll): presence, superb communication, and exquisite empathy. So it is not about novelty or rose petals, fancy positions or role plays, but the most longed-for and most tragically missing ingredients in the neglect experience, and in the world, really. What a magnificent world it would be if we all cultivated and practiced those three! So, there you have it. As Rabbi Hillel would say, "Now go and study!"

The welcome earworm in my head jumping into 2023 and the Year of the Rabbit is John and Yoko's timeless 1969 classic Give Peace a Chance. "All we are saying is give peace a chance..." I would take it even further and add "Give Magnificence a Chance" (And my own additional verse, "Give Sleep a Chance!")

Kung Hei Fat Choi!

 Ruth Cohn

02 ——————

Glorious?

"Dickkopf,"
Com Panis, Meanings

We saw so few movies when we were growing up that the ones we did see stick in my mind, like the 1968 film Oliver!, the film version of the musical based on the classic Dickens novel, Oliver Twist. The bits I remember about it were how the boys, victims of child slave labor, shared beds. one sleeping during the other's 12-hour work shift, and the song "Food, Glorious Food!" The boys were so hungry they dreamed of food and sang joyously about what they craved. I remember a bittersweet feeling about that song. Although food was certainly plentiful enough in our house, it was, to me, anything but glorious. It was more on the order of a protracted, hideous, recurring nightmare.

I was always dickkopf (fathead) and a bad eater. I did not like meat, which made for an ongoing power struggle. Now I am not a formal vegetarian, meaning I have no ethical, political or spiritual rationale; it's simply my age-old distaste/preference to avoid meat.

Meal times were not much fun, anyway. Our dad, who had been a chef before becoming a cantor, repeatedly told Mom with a smile, "I did not marry you for your cooking," but really, it was no joke. When he cooked, he required a fair measure of adulation for the uppity French dishes he made, which were never my taste, apart from the meat issue. There was also a truly unsavory period of at least several years that I think of as the "Kosher wars." Our dad wanted to keep a kosher kitchen, and Mom wouldn't do it.

He lived on nightly Hebrew National hot dogs until she finally relented with, "OK, I will cook what you buy." I don't remember how they resolved the part about two sets of dishes. Mostly I remember the long and bitter tension that hung heavily over our family table. No great surprise when my trauma expressed itself via, among the many other symptoms, a near-fatal anorexia that spanned my adolescence, but really much more. In 1967, anorexia and eating disorders in general were even less understood than they are now. There was no treatment to speak of, and I was simply viewed as a "bad girl", creating headaches for my parents. I somehow got to a healthy-ish weight eventually, but the agony of obsession persisted for decades.

After many years and all sorts of somatic approaches alongside my depth psychotherapy, I can say food is one of the truly glorious and great pleasures of my life. I love it and am grateful to say I eat whatever I want. I love making food, too. I am a home cheesemaker, a sourdough baker, and I aspire to grow vegetables when I can make the time. On a particularly bad day at the office, I might rant to my ever-patient partner, "I'm done! I am going to retire, be a cheesemaker!" until I calm down. We do, however, love our food.

Com Panis

When I was in the throes of my eating disorder, our dad would rail at me that the word companion emerged from the Latin com panis, sharing bread. Eating together was a natural and human way to connect. Ideally, that would be true. My not wanting to was somehow inhuman. For so many who grew up in a household of trauma and neglect, it was decidedly not a way to connect, and disordered eating is a not-so-uncommon expression of dysregulation.

I was interested to learn that, in a strange way, the whole category of com panis and food culture became a mechanism of social control and an attempt at cultural change in the Soviet Union. I heard an interesting story, "Dissident Kitchens", on one of those wonderful late-night Public Radio programs. After the revolution in 1917, food was scarce. The new Stalinist government set about industrializing food, The foods to be eaten were determined by the government, and everyone ate the same. Private kitchens were considered bourgeois. New apartments were built without kitchens.

Rather, there were large communal kitchens, and people broke their bread in dining halls with 500 comrades. The Bolsheviks were not interested in the tradition or the aesthetic of food. First, food shortages devastated all that, but further, private kitchens were considered "bourgeois." The foods to be eaten were determined by the government, and everyone ate the same. Apparently, and understandably, the people hated that and sorely missed cooking and the ritual of sharing intimate family mealtimes.

When Kruschev replaced the Stalinist regime in 1953, to address the housing shortage, he had apartments built once again with small kitchens, which became a place for families and friends to gather. Now, cookbooks and programs reflect the slow and steady revival and reclamation of traditional Russian foods. And although Russia is currently alienating many of us, its food story is informative, and reminds us how very elemental the family table is. Eating together in harmony is on the order of a birthright. And the way it is corrupted in micro and macro forms of trauma is a crime against nature as far as I am concerned!

Meanings

One of my favorite books of all time is Michael Pollan's epic Omnivore's Dilemma, which approaches food from myriad directions: psychological, emotional, nutritional, environmental, political, cultural, ethical, aesthetic, historical... what else? Long before he became a harbinger and champion of psychedelics, Pollan wrote brilliantly and prolifically about food and its many meanings, which span quite a universe. There is even now an emerging sub-field of culinary medicine, which makes a lot of sense to me. Here in San Francisco, food is virtually on the order of religion, which can be both a pleasure and an embarrassment.

The dysregulations of trauma and neglect that manifest as disordered eating are some of the most persistent and challenging to heal. I have worked with survivors who suffered disordered eating of every stripe, not to mention my own. I do not pretend to know how to treat eating disorders effectively, and I have yet to see programs that do. Please prove me wrong! The best thing I know, which is the best thing I know for trauma in general, is the combination of depth, attachment-oriented psychotherapy, and neurofeedback. If I had had that 50 years ago, who knows if my own healing would have required less than the multiple decades it did?

Whatever we can do to get the shame out, even better. And whatever we can do to break the intergenerational transmission not only of trauma, but also the agony of interference with the natural development of food and eating tastes and habits, better still. It is my wish that "enlightened feeding," becomes an aspect of "enlightened parenting." Although I am not a mother, I am indeed a proverbial "Jewish mother" in that I love to make and give food, although certainly not to foist unwanted food on anyone ever! Far be that from me! But for me, it can be an exquisite show of love and care, as long as (like with any gift!) the recipient is truly seen, known, and considered.

Our mom used to say "Mahlzeit!" before we ate. I never knew what it meant, thinking it was "mouse-ite." I picture a little family of mice enjoying their dinner (maybe cheese?) It is a form of greeting and celebratory marking of mealtime. We later evolved into singing a Hebrew grace before meals. Although I have long since given that up, I do like the ritual of feeling and acknowledging with gratitude before we eat. My husband graciously does all the grocery shopping, buying those things that I am not able to make for us myself. My little ritual has become a hug and a loud exclamation, "I love you! Thanks for the food!" What's yours?

Enjoy your dinner!

03

Outside the Lines:

Time, Art, Hope

Although I am committed to no rushing, I am rarely successful. I am always trying to do too much in a day; the time gets away from me. I wind up feeling disappointed about all that I did not get done and wondering, where does the time go? I have no idea where it went, and there is never enough. It is hard to remember the long, lonely years when the time weighed so heavily on my hands as to be unbearable. Getting through the day was like pushing Sisyphus' leaden boulder, invariably feeling it refuse to move. I thought there was something wrong with the clock. Now I know the amygdala has no time: the trauma brain simply cannot tell the difference between past and present.

Neglect is a bleak, empty cavernous void. I imagine an infant lying alone in a darkened room, helpless, with no way of knowing if anyone will ever come, let alone when. I am often visited by that image when sitting with a client who describes their days as interminable, desolate, powerless, and hopeless. I have no doubt that is how it was. What is so insidious about trauma healing is that experience is not remembered but relived. Being one of absences, holes in time, empty space, and no story to remember, the neglect story is a reliving of that. Often accompanied by a panoply of somatic mystery symptoms, it is puzzling. People often ask me, "Why do I feel so much worse than ever? When is this going to end?," the musing of the young child, I imagine, who, of course, does not have the words.

I remember watching out the window, counting cars. I must have been six because that window was in the house in South Bend, and I knew how to count. I was counting and waiting for Daddy's Chevy to pull in and for him to bound in the door, calling out, "Ho ho!" Why did I look forward to that? I don't know; I do know it was invariably a long wait. I remember one time when I fasted for two weeks, with only a bit of water now and then. I called it the Long March. I would count the hours as meal times would come and pass. There was lunch, check. There was dinner, check. Day one, day two, up to fourteen. How did I do that? I don't remember. I remember later watching the clock not move, waiting to get to the magic hour of 4:45 when I could crack my bottle of Old Crow, a $6.95 a quart rotgut bourbon. It worked; I got through the day. I remember that old song by John and Yoko, "Whatever gets you through the night, is alright"

The healing years can be slower, longer, and arguably even worse than the original trauma experience, especially because it makes no sense. "I am worse than before! Is this therapy making me worse?" I wondered, and people ask me. It is hard to provide an answer that makes any difference. The best I can do is hold the certainty that I know it will, and I do. That is why I always say everything I have ever been through serves me.

Art

I have always loved art. I love pretty things, I love looking at art, I love making things, and I love beauty. I can say I love visual beauty more than music, maybe. Like many of my era, I idealized the iconic Frida Kahlo. She had terrible trauma and physical pain, but she managed it most successfully by painting prolifically, mostly graphic and dramatic self-portraits. Bright, primary colors, realism and symbolism, tragedy but also the beauty of nature, flowers, birds, animals, even hope. She found her way, and even with the ongoing trauma of her brilliant and cheating husband, she prevailed. Her life never ceased to be hard, but her powerful work is a legacy and an inspiration to many, especially women.

During the worst of those interminable years, probably after I finally surrendered alcohol to start trudging the rugged road of recovery, I don't remember how I started to draw. I used colored pencils, never having the patience for unwieldy media and needing to feel a sense of control. I drew myself, largely rendering from old photos of many ages, but my family members too. I had my own symbology of icons and monsters that recurred. I sat, and I drew and drew and drew, and it gobbled up the time. There was no clock, there were no meals to track. I was in what that famous Hungarian guy with the unpronounceable name called flow. I was amazed; my artistry was very good. It has never been that good since.

So much story was unearthed and even processed in those long hours at the kitchen table. I would roll up the large sheets and take them to therapy to review them with the witness, my therapist. I wonder how much more quickly things would have moved if I had had neurofeedback then. Quite a few years later, when EMDR came on the scene, and I was studying and practicing that, I had an EMDR therapist who was also an art therapist. I can't remember how she combined them, but it was a good idea. I am sure it was good, at least at the time. I don't remember much. However, nothing was again like those hours at the kitchen table.

I still have the drawings, sheaves of them, in large, now ragged brown cardboard portfolios. They trailed with me through all of my vagabond moves over decades. I don't look at them often, but they are a record of where I was, that long slog. They certainly keep me grateful. My best friend was in film school at that time, and made a movie with my drawings about the power of art for healing. She recently had the VHS converted to DVD. Now, if I could just find my DVD attachment, I'd like to have another look!

Hope

This was actually intended to be a missive of hope. I am not sure if it came across that way! Trauma and neglect are like a childhood of wild scribbles, not the orderly coloring book of a safe childhood. Of course, healing will be largely outside the lines, sometimes wildly so. My artwork was not cheery, but the colors are strong and have stood the test of time, as has the rocky but persistent healing work. Sometimes I feel as if my main task is a hope monger, to keep the faith somehow. I still occasionally have days where I have to be that for myself. That's OK. Now I know that the clock is not broken; time does not really stand still, or at least not for long. And I agree with John and Yoko, whatever gets you through the night, is alright.... well, as long as you don't do any harm to yourself or another. Colored pencils are definitely better than bourbon or starvation.

Cheese is an excellent teacher. The Monterey Jack I made last week required 70 minutes of stirring. That's right! I stand on my little stool, stirring my 8-gallon pot for that long. I get to watch a whole lot of great webinars! The aging time is another story. I remember when I first started making cheese, and the idea of waiting four months before it was ready seemed like a cruel joke. Now four is a short time; a good Parmesan or cheddar will take a year or more. Gardening is the same way. I used to grow roses when I lived in Berkeley. I read that when you grow asparagus, it takes eight years before you get a crop! The waiting is part of the protocol, part of the deal. Hard to metabolize that some of these invaluable processes are simply not to be hurried. Some of those cheeses really stink! But we find them delicious.

04

Apartheid Redux:

Re-enactment,
Fragmentation, Integration

Rest in peace

WARNING: *This blog includes graphic content that may be disturbing to some readers.*

I suppose by now it is naive to be shocked by yet another traffic-stop murder of a young Black man. The death of Tyre Nichols, however, flooded me with feelings. We have been barraged by mass shootings here in California, with a tally of 19 dead in the space of 44 hours this month. But in this case, as in the case of George Floyd, the murder was flesh on flesh: knee to neck, flying fists, feet, and batons against body – something about how visceral, how undisguisedly vulnerable, human ,and inhuman it was, is particularly chilling about Nichols'murder. I most intentionally do not watch the videos, but what others tell me is how fiercely, vividly out of control the five officers seemed, like the frenzied scenes in the classic novel Lord of the Flies that haunted me back when I first read it almost 60 years ago. In this case, it was Black flesh on Black flesh, which makes about as much sense as parents or spouses brutalizing their own flesh and blood or their intimate partners.

There is a legacy, a heritage, of centuries of brutal beatings in this country and remembered in the Black body: centuries of slavery, Jim Crow, Rodney King in 1991, so many traumatic generations of transmission. The fact that this murder was perpetrated by African American officers does not make it any less a racist crime. This case shows us how the lack of trauma-informed healing, education, and policy morphs into more crime. It is a horrifying reminder of the essential nature of our work. As we know, trauma is not remembered but relived, and tragically often re-enacted. Not always, of course, and thankfully, but often enough – way too much, really.

Re-enactment

One of many reasons I have found couples' therapy with survivors of trauma and neglect so compelling is because of how dramatically and even explicitly the trauma stories make themselves known. I always say to my clients (and sometimes my husband!), "Nothing is activating like the intimate partnership!" Perhaps the couple is as family-like as any relationship, so we regroup the trauma family in this new configuration, and it becomes the stage for the story to unwittingly unfold. The couple's therapist sees dynamics and often well-hidden aspects of a person that the individual therapist might never see or imagine. Clients do get angry or shut down with the individual therapist and to greater or lesser extents the transference projections appear. Regrettably, I do know that my husband has seen the worst of me like no one else has, and as a result, the fact that he is still there makes him a reassuring beacon of safety like I have never known. Those couples who stay the course get to enjoy that outcome too. This is not to say that I never lapse into, usually and hopefully, momentary states of unbidden memory. But I/we become much more able to find our way back to the prefrontal cortex fairly quickly. And yes, long and diligent work is required.

It continues to amaze me how diametrically, stunningly, my perceptions can become distorted, even now. If there is something I am particularly uncertain or insecure about, my lens perceiving judgment and rejection under every rock zooms into the forefront, like when I hit the zoom in option on my View menu and the whole screen leaps out at me. Suddenly I am that little godforsaken neglected girl again who can't trust anyone, whom everyone is out to get, as our dad would say, and I am unshakably believing it. Reassuring words annoy me, rolling off like water off a duck's back. Often all that is required is settling the addled nervous system or simple rest. After some gentle and nourishing sleep or a nice long stir of the cheese vat, the whole world looks different. I can see the exaggeration and distortion and find compassion for whomever I may have villainized or projected onto. Of course, usually, there is a kernel of something to pay attention to in real-time, but it is no longer catastrophic as it had seemed when I was activated. So simple, and yet how messed up the world becomes without... Oy vey!

Yes, even now, I am visited by episodes, but I can generally keep from embarrassing myself, recognize them reasonably quickly, and locate the MIA prefrontal cortex, where my self-knowledge, good sense, and generosity live. The more work we do, the quicker the turnaround, which is why I am such a stickler for doing the work, and staying the course, whatever that might mean in your lexicon.

Life is infinitely less dangerous now, at least in the interpersonal field, which was always the most volatile (and generally is for those with trauma and neglect – at least those of us privileged enough to live in the First World or where there is not a literal war going on). Now I do, in fact, have the previously unthinkable: support, places to turn, and even internal resources.

Integration

Sometimes, it really seems like some interior version of Apartheid, a polarity between Me and Not Me, or a split self. One can think I am crazy or schizophrenic, or who is that? Like the old game show "Truth or Consequences," where the contestants had to guess which person was the real one of the three. It seems to me in the trauma field, we used to talk about it more: the fragmentation of the self. We described the self as fractured self between hyperarousal"\ and numbing, limbic versus prefrontal: dissociation. Maybe it is my imagination, but we don't seem to use that language much anymore. In that "other " state, we seem to turn into someone else. I wonder who those five Black cops were as children, as spouses, as targeted young Black men themselves, and what inhabited them and took them over to flip into such monsters? This is not to excuse them in any way, but to remind us that it is our duty to the world, as well as ourselves and known loved ones, to do our work, and to help others do theirs so we don't continue this hellish chain of trauma, neglect, injustice, and insanity.

I date myself as I remember growing up hearing about the Iron Curtain and the Berlin Wall, dramatic bifurcations on a mass scale. My childhood image of the Iron Curtain was of a larger-than-life chain mail shower curtain encircling the huge amoeba-like shape of Russia on the map.

The massive brick wall dividing family from family in Berlin was easier to picture. The fracture of self was in the daily news. It made no sense, but it was familiar. How do we get anywhere if we cannot even knit back together what was once (hopefully) singular? Again, we must, of course, start with ourselves, then work with our partners and families, and our communities, and finally the world.

Evolutionary biologists remind us that inclusion is a survival need. As mammals, as pack animals, without it, we die. When we fear we are, or actually are, outside, we go into the extremes of self-preservation-terror and flee, or fight all too often, and we end up with a messed-up world.

"Not one more!" is the cry both about senseless murders, civil wars, and ravaged, traumatized, neglected selves. Let's unite around that!

05 ———

Not Me:
Repurposing, Rejecting, Renaming

When I was in kindergarten and first grade in New York City, teachers had not yet made the rule that we had to give Valentine's cards to everyone in the class. We all had our little art project mailboxes made out of decorated brown paper bags perched expectantly on the sides of our desks. The popular kids' bags brimmed over with the bright red missives of love. Invariably mine was, as Tony Soprano would say, a little light. I felt like a reject or a queer, back when that word was not associated with sexual orientation but rather with being weird and outcast. By the time they made the rule about inclusion, it was way too late for my battered ego. I knew that the kids only stuffed my mailbox because they had to. I would have felt like a reject anyway because that is how a child internalizes neglect. I am ignored because I'm worthless, or worse.

As I got older, I was so used to being a misfit, an introvert, and later a rebel, that I did not get caught in the romance around Valentine's Day. But I certainly saw the big build-up and letdown among so many of the kids around me. Valentine's Day can be a dreaded nightmare for many who are unpartnered and often even worse for those that are.

As a couples' therapist, working with many clients who have histories of childhood trauma and neglect, I am faced daily with major disconnects and misunderstandings between them about what makes both of them feel loved, and giving and receiving. Valentine's Day can be a veritable hornet's nest for both, resulting in major ruptures and hurt feelings that endure like the ghosts of Valentine's Day past.

This year I had an idea to help my struggling couples. In anticipation of the potentially spikey day, I thought, how about if we head it off with a conversation or two about what makes you feel loved. I still feel shame about my ungracious response to a beautiful gift my husband had picked out and bought for me over 25 years ago. I was convinced he bought that instead of the printer I wanted for my computer out of stinginess. It was only much later that I learned that the gift he had bought me, a set of Italian ceramic canisters for my baking ingredients, cost at least five times as much as the lowly printer I had requested. I still have the canisters, and besides being a lovely home for my various flours, they are a ready reminder that I do have the power to inflict great hurt.

The child of neglect can readily believe that only someone who matters has the power to inflict harm, to be mean. Someone inconsequential is not important enough to injure another. Not! It is a myth essential to be corrected and healed for the sake of all involved!

For many, What makes me feel loved? is a hard question to answer, even about oneself. If I don't know, I certainly can't communicate it intelligibly to my partner, who may be trying and failing, and lapsing into hopelessness, impatience, frustration, and ultimately, anger. If pleasing me is enough of a moving target, of course, they will give up in fatigue and despair. Then I can insist I was right! I am simply not worth the trouble. I have the insidious power to fulfill my own bitter prophecy.

Rejecting

At the core of childhood neglect is the often unremembered and nonetheless indelible experience or perception of rejection. It is a ready and "logical" interpretation for a seemingly chronic lack of attention or priority: I am unwanted, unworthy, undesirable, unlovable. And it is a "handy" default that can readily slide, often before they even know it, into withdrawal, sulkiness, or even unwitting rejection of others.

I remember my therapist saying to me years ago, with that sledgehammer voice she sometimes used to get through my thick cloud of triggered mud, "You're the rejector!"

I did not get it – when I shut down as impenetrably as Fort Knox after a perceived slight, a whiff of dislike, complaint, or judgment towards me, I am the rejector.

I did not recognize that what I thought of as my self-protection or quiet scream of "Leave me alone!" could be experienced as harshness or even hostility. Frankly, it simply did not occur to me that I could have an impact. Again, that is the mark of neglect. Whatever the child might do to attract or garner the loving attention they crave does not work. I never imagined that I could be mean or rejecting. Not me!

Valentine's Day can indeed pose special challenges for the child of neglect of any age. The core dilemma surrounding neglect is the gnawing ambivalence about interpersonal connection.
There is, to a varying degree, the quaking ache of longing for closeness in a fierce tug of war with the terror and even rage around abandonment and loss. It can be a persistant plague that might feel or seem unresolvable. I used to berate myself with, "I simply can't get along with humans." Many survivors of neglect tend to people their relationship world with animals instead. I have long since joyfully and gratefully proven myself wrong. It is not an easy journey, but imminently possible and definitely worth it.

I have also learned that when neglect survivor clients seem viciously rejecting of me, they may really be wishing I might find them in their hiding place, or perhaps unwittingly showing me how it was.

Another of Valentine's Day challenges has to do with gifts, as in the case of my canister set. It may be a day when we hope or wish for a particular gift from that special person: flowers, chocolates, or something personal. Gifts can embody the dilemma of the child of neglect: If I permit you to get it right, do I run the risk of puncturing my wall of solitude and self-reliance? Without realizing it, one may become the rejector. I always say thatIt takes humility to receive a gift, to let the other know what would indeed hit the mark, and make me feel loved.

There is no one right, normal, or best expression of love. I encourage us all to examine our own 'not me;' let others know what makes us feel loved, and give love a chance!

Renaming

In 1988, the renowned author and playwright Eve Ensler had the idea of rebranding February 14 as V Day, V being for vulva or vagina. In conjunction with her historic theater piece the Vagina Monologues, which rocked the world, it was to be a day devoted to ending violence against women, girls, and the planet,. Ensler subsequently changed her name to V.

Transforming or expanding the focus and intent of Valentine's Day is a fine idea! To teach our loved ones how they can effectively communicate love to us and thereby break the chain of rejection is a way of eradicating at least some measure of violence. Betty Dodson, champion of the female orgasm, was known for saying, "Viva la Vulva!"

Thanks, Betty! Thanks, V! And Happy V Day to all!

06

Solar Eclipse:

Existence, Fame, Ambivalen

What I remember best about John F. Kennedy's assassination is the looping image of the president's little son, John-John, saluting as his father's coffin passed. In 1963, I was eight, and we lived in South Bend, Indiana, where the winters were fierce and long. I was hunkered down in the basement, with the heat blasting and unending coverage of the memorial and the national tragedy on TV non-stop. That image of John-John must have replayed a million times – or maybe it is the distortion of my young memory and my profound identification with the grief-stricken child. I don't remember much else about John Kennedy Junior through the rest of my life, but I never forgot when he was, I guess, three.

The Kennedys were iconized, as tragedy and martyrdom often are, and it was years before I knew some of the unsavory politics and aspects of JFK's life. I was surprised a few days ago when I heard a story memorializing his sister Rosemary Kennedy on the 18th anniversary of her death.

I did not know there was a Kennedy sibling who had been lobotomized for being slow. It got me thinking about the neglect, even seeming annihilation, that often comes with political or other kinds of greatness, large and small.

Our dad was not a major celebrity or famous, but as a religious and community leader, he was a he was a public figure of sorts. I remember when we were growing up, sometimes when we met someone new, someone he knew, or someone noteworthy, he would say, "Do they know who you are?" The emphasis on are meant, "Do they know you are my daughter? The cantor's daughter?" Evidently, that was all that I was. There was no me.

When our mom died, we each had a list of people to call and notify, One of the people on my list was the teacher of Dad's autobiography writing group. He had been in that group for perhaps five years, writing and sharing his memoir. Everyone loved him. Apparently, the group format was that participants would read aloud and comment on each other's work, so they knew each other quite well after that long. When I identified myself to the teacher, she said, "Oh! I didn't know he had a daughter." Rather shocked, (but not really) I said, "Yes. He has three." As ever, my existence was an ongoing question. In this case, it was all three of us.

I remember early on feeling I had to justify my existence somehow, to earn my right to occupy a patch of ground to stand on, on this earth. Much of the time, I felt like a puff of smoke or shadow that was perhaps punctuation in his screenplay, or a prop or extra in his movie. Perhaps that is why I excised the word deserve from my personal lexicon, and to this day, I bristle when I hear it. There really is no such thing in this world as deserving, or perhaps more accurately, getting what one deserves – so I believed.

In the mind of the neglected child, existence is a mystery, or it was to me. Worthiness, merit, privilege, specialness, responsibility, luck-- how do they all fit together? How is it determined who gets what? Why me? Or why not me and what on earth to do about it? I remember early in my exploration and study of neglect, I could spot a child of neglect quickly by the signature shrug, deep as the ocean, of "I don't know what to do!" or "There is nothing I can do!"

Fame

Nelson Mandela was quoted as saying, "I have
often wondered whether a person is justified in
neglecting his own family for opportunities to fight
for others." Mandela's daughter Maki, as much as
she admires her father, recounts painful memories
of not knowing if he loved her or not. These
memories are from long before her father was
in hiding or imprisoned, She is torn by grief and
bitterness about her devastating neglect, tugging
against profound feelings of admiration, respect,
and pride. "I had a father who was not there –
which was how I saw it through the eyes of a child
– who chose politics over me or even my brothers,
my family." I heard similar sentiments expressed by
her brother in an interview some years ago, but I
can't seem to find it now.

Fidel Castro's oldest son, also named Fidel, was a
prominent physicist and accomplished researcher.
He died by suicide at the age of 68. I don't know
the details. What are the unique costs and conflicts
of being the child of greatness, of being eclipsed by
the world's suffering? How does a child make sense
of, or peace with that through their lifespan?

Our dad did much good in his own particular sphere. Like Mandela, our father was never around. On weekends, I wished he would come home, but he was often running to the hospital to visit congregants. I could not begin to compete with the sick, dying, and grieving multitudes. It is a mitzvah, a good deed, to visit the sick, a noble and generous act of charity. I honored and respected, even learned from that. But I, guiltily, hated it, and shame on me for feeling that!

Ambivalence

Neglect is fraught with searing, seemingly irreconcilable ambivalences. There are mixed feelings of jealousy versus guilt, rage, and resentment versus social and political responsibility, grief versus gratitude, love versus bitterness, self-care versus greater good, gratitude versus tail-chasing confusion. I am still flummoxed about the balance between my commitment to the larger world and looking out for my little and aging self.

Neglect is fraught with searing, seemingly irreconcilable ambivalences. There are mixed feelings of jealousy versus guilt, rage, and resentment versus social and political responsibility, grief versus gratitude, love versus bitterness, self-care versus greater good, gratitude versus tail-chasing confusion. I am still flummoxed about the balance between my commitment to the larger world and looking out for my little and aging self. I admit that is part of what keeps me awake at night. My feelings about our dad are in a similarly vacillating: both/and. He, perhaps, hurt me more than anyone, but he also bequeathed to me all of my most cherished traits, qualities, and many skills. How do I resolve that? How do I make sense of it? What do I call it? That, of course, complicated my feelings further as his life drew to a close, now almost three years ago.

Thankfully, I do not suffer about it anymore – it is more a contemplation.

I sometimes wonder: is the price of heroism, martyrdom, or goodness the sacrifice of one's kids? Kids have no say, no voice. Are they/we part of the deal? Sadly, it is on the unconsenting child to figure it out, to deal with the fallout of the neglect. Perhaps that is the conundrum that plagues a lifetime?

I have always been puzzled by the Bible story in which God instructs Abraham to sacrifice his son as a show of faith. Dylan eloquently expressed my sentiments in his timeless song, "Highway 61": "Abe said God, you must be puttin me on." I didn't get it. How is that a good thing? I don't know. I have had a similar conflict with an occasional client who had a famous parent whom I had always iconized and admired, until being jarred by a back story of a casualty that I had not known about before; or after reading a memoir by the child of a hero figure who may have caused devastating harm. Steve Jobs' first daughter Lisa asked, "Was I named after the computer or was the computer named after me?!" I don't know if she ever resolved it. I still struggle with the ongoing choice between my own interests and the larger good. Perhaps it will always be one of those chicken-and-egg scenarios.

07

Half the Sky:
Valor, Grief, Transformation

Back when I was in college, I remember the Maoists used to say, "Women hold up half the sky." Although I was never a Maoist, I always loved this image of women, muscled arms upstretched, supporting at least half of this wide world of ours. As we approach International Women's Day, it continues to shock me that girls and women can still be prohibited from going to school; imprisoned and even killed over what they wear or their reproductive decisions in 2023. In some parts of the world, perhaps more than others, the sky is falling.

In honor of International Women's Day, I want to memorialize a quiet and powerfully important woman who equally quietly slipped away on February 3, 2023. She was only 79, and I say only because the numbers seem smaller and smaller as I approach them myself. I say quietly because after hearing through the grapevine that she had passed, I systematically combed the web and all my accessible resources, and turned up nothing: no obituary or substantial biographical material. Finally, an article written by her husband made the rounds and landed in my inbox. The woman is, or was, Sue Othmer, the valiant matriarch of neurofeedback.

I am moved to write about Sue, not only because neurofeedback is so powerful as a way of working with developmental trauma, neglect, and many other afflictions, but also because she epitomizes the polar opposite of the neglectful mother.

Her life and career were inspired, shaped, and compelled by her fierce attention and commitment to the thriving, healthy, and safe development of her children.

Born in Boston, Sue, then Fitzgerald, grew up in Anchorage, Alaska and later Bethesda, Maryland. A superior achiever in school, she later studied physics and then neurobiology at Cornell and then at Oxford, where she met her husband and later professional partner, Siegfried Othmer. They were married for 52 years. In 1968, their first child Brian was born, followed in 1973 by their daughter Karen, and then in 1975, Kurt.

Grief

Grief was both the context and the catalyst of Sue's life; certainly her professional life. Karen died at 14 months of a brain tumor. At the time of his sister's death, Brian had already been suffering from painful mental and behavioral problems for five years. As time went on, Brian's complex problems evolved further into a difficult-to-treat seizure disorder.

The Othmers set out on a fervent quest in search of help and relief for Brian, in the course of which Sue happened upon a then new procedure developed by Barry Sterman at UCLA: neurofeedback. Sterman had been experimenting and succeeding at curing seizures in cats. The Othmers were heartened to find that neurofeedback proved helpful to Brian as well. And although it was not sufficient to save him, it gave him six good years, enabling him, almost, to graduate from college before his death in 1991. By the age of 47, the Othmers had lost two children. By then, however, Sue had studied and created an evolving mental health treatment option of neurofeedback. Transforming her own tragedy, she made a tremendous contribution to the world and certainly to my life and work.

I only had the occasion to meet Sue once. It was probably in 2009. I was a starry-eyed neurofeedback practitioner, fresh out of my beginners' training. For some reason, neurofeedback did not seem to have caught hold on the West Coast of the US: strange because I have always thought of my coast, particularly the San Francisco Bay Area, as being in the vanguard of the new and groundbreaking of whatever discipline.(My impression is it still hasn't, much to my dismay and despite my humble efforts to disseminate it,) In those days, I traveled wherever I had to and wherever I could to learn more. When the Othmers offered a weekend workshop in Los Angeles, I was on it in a hot minute.

Sadly, the neurofeedback field, mighty but small, has been fractured by factionalism and infighting. As my consultant once said, "The polar bears get on well when there is plenty of salmon. However, when there is not enough salmon, they fight among themselves." So unfortunately, this discipline suffers from a senseless otherism. While needing numbers and unity to garner attention and research funding, practitioners could not settle enough on a unified purpose to work together. So be it; I did not know that then. When I enthusiastically found myself in the Othmers' training, I did not know I had crossed lines. But it did not matter.

I don't remember that weekend well, but I do remember that I loved it. Sue was a towering, if somewhat quiet, exquisitely smart, strong, precise, and no-nonsense presence. Although not warm or approachable, I liked and admired her, and she was a fine teacher. She gracefully held up her half of the sky alongside her powerful and imposing husband and professional partner. Indeed, they were the highly effective neurofeedback power couple.

Neurofeedback has continued to evolve and grow into an increasingly comprehensive, complex, and effective methodology beneficial to so many people (and some animals!) who have a broad spectrum of somatic, emotional, and behavioral symptoms. It combines science, art, and perhaps some magic,. all in a sea of hope, tireless conviction, and hard work. All of these epitomized Sue Othmer.

Again, while I am not religious; I have little puffs of memory that float up from my childhood of compulsory religious school. I remember the song, the quote from Proverbs: "A woman of valor who can find? Her price is more precious than rubies" That does sound like Sue.

In many ways, a simple procedure (simple enough
to be used successfully on cats!) neurofeedback
is also vastly complex, and learning it is endless.
It works on the principle of operant conditioning,
which seems utterly obvious, but can be so easily
forgotten. Positive feedback is re-enforcing: reward,
encouragement, acknowledgment, appreciating
all the positives, strengthening, and increasing
whatever behavior or change is being rewarded.
It seems like a no-brainer. I will resist the urge to
rhapsodize about neurofeedback here, but I will
surely return to it repeatedly. And there is much
information to be found about neurofeedback!

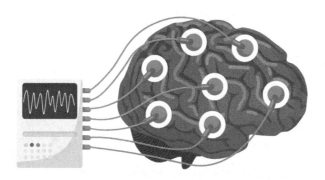

Even More Late Night Contemplations About Trauma and Neglect

Transformation

From the ravaging flames of grief, from the depths of her broken heart, Sue Othmer summoned the mythical phoenix of neurofeedback. She and Siegfried continued to experiment, study, evolve, and teach it until she could not, creating new and even more mysterious iterations, but never flagging in her curiosity, vision, and energy. I know how much neurofeedback has regulated, healed, and enhanced my own life, and that of my many clients over the past 14 years, as well as countless suffering people around the world. It certainly guided the direction my own practice has taken, and I am so grateful.

So often tragedy and grief, pain and suffering spawn and catalyze immense creativity and inspiration. This is not to minimize or cancel out the impact of loss, violence, or destruction, but perhaps to give them meaning. I have always said that everything I have ever been through serves me. That certainly cannot be said of all trauma. But I am vastly grateful to all the many who have made a gift to us all of their own agonies. Thanks, Sue, and Happy International Women's Day to all!

08

To Be or Not to Be:

Love? Presence, Attachment

Occasionally, I read a book because it has been hanging out on the New York Times Bestseller List for so long that I feel I need to know what everyone is reading to keep up with the times. No, I am not talking about The Body Keeps the Score, which has been a fixture on the list for seemingly ever! (I was probably one of the first people to read that!) I did read 50 Shades of Gray (all three volumes!) only for that reason. Sometimes I do it also because the book was recommended by someone I am very fond of. Recently a very intelligent young friend recommended a book that has been persistently hovering out there for quite a while, so I decided to go for it: the memoir I'm Glad My Mom Died by Jennette McCurdy. Born in 1992, she became a child TV star by eight.

Never much of a TV watcher, and also of the wrong generation to be familiar with her, McCurdy's story was new to me. I had never heard of the many shows she appeared in. But I found the book interesting because it is an exquisite portrayal of an often unrecognized and devastating form of neglect.

Growing up in a Mormon household, she was the youngest of four, the only girl, the most adored child, and wildly idealized by her clearly troubled mother. McCurdy's mother, Debra, had always dreamed of being a movie or TV star herself, and she painstakingly molded and sculpted Jennette to become the child star of her own lost aspirational dreams. Right from the start, Debra dressed, coiffed, and shaped Jennette's appearance, and even play, to be Little Debra 2.0, but the deluxe version that had never materialized for her.

Until her earlyish adulthood, Jennette experiences her mother's attention and focus as the epitome of love. They were inseparable and Jennette lived to please her mother, while her mother busily doted on and prepped her daughter to inhabit the illusion. They did everything together, including creating and sharing perversely disordered eating that would train little Jennette to aspire to anorexic weights and sizes, well before she received that indoctrination from the larger world. It was their little shared ritual to go out to lunch and split a chef's salad with the dressing on the side, no cheese, no meat, and no egg. Debra was able to locate and ultimately enlist the connections and the professionals that would connect little Jennette with first extra, then guest, and then starring regular roles in ongoing TV shows. Debra was thrilled, triumphant and proud, as well as relieved by the ways that Jenette's income took the financial pressure off the otherwise struggling family.

Having survived, at least into remission, a serious bout of cancer, Debra was able to utilize the cancer card to win sympathy and the occasional pass,, to get her way both inside and outside the family. Debra was the super-nova. Jennette was but a satellite. This kind of neglect, where there is no you, is one of the most devastating and insidious. The child is told and imagines she is so loved that the annihilation and, in effect, soul murder, not to mention the extreme of intrusion, are indiscernible to the young person. It takes a while for the rage to register, for the authentic, inaudible voice of "What about me?" to emerge. And who is "me," anyway?

It is only when Jennette was sidling into adulthood that she began to feel tired and resentful of living out her mother's dream, of being her mother's alter-ego. By then, she was completely dysregulated, struggling with severely disordered eating, well on her way to alcoholism, and of course, experiences every kind of relationship and sexual confusion. It is a devastatingly brilliant portrayal of a profound, unrecognized form of neglect/attachment trauma.

It would have been unthinkable for Jennette to imagine herself being neglected, as the attention, preoccupation, and obsession with her was unrelenting. Like many who are nominally loved even with less extreme of intrusion, it is challenging to identify the loss of self and the profound destruction of not being known, understood, or seen.

Presence

Although Jennette rarely had a moment free of Debra's invasion into any space she found herself in, her mother was never present with her. That invaluably vital developmental ingredient of being truly there with her never happened. Many clients I have seen bear all the scars of neglect but are hard-pressed to recognize, let alone name, their experience of nonexistence, of not being seen or known. They can't understand why they feel so bad, shamefully calling it a failure of gratitude or some other sort of personal failure. Sometimes, their only identifiable and barely legitimate complaint (to them) might be in bodily symptoms.

Jennette's eating disorder is florid and undeniable, and she portrays the mysterious swings between anorexia and terrifying, uncontrollable binge eating as well as I have ever read. She exquisitely describes being out of control with not eating, and then as uncontrollably swinging the other way and being unable to stop eating. Although thankfully, I never "graduated" to bulimia the way she did, I remember that runaway train. It is a nightmare I hate to remember. How courageously and graphically she exposes it! It helps her to recognize that something is truly wrong. Sometimes only the body can communicate this or force it into awareness, as we are all finally starting to understand.

I was recently reminded of the unspeakable power of simple presence. I had a minor surgery that required anesthesia and I was still pretty drugged on the car ride home and our return to the house. Apparently, it was early afternoon when my husband delivered us safely home. My memory is spotty to blank for most of it. I floated through the afternoon in a deep sleep and woke up somewhat disoriented about what day or time it was. Opening my eyes, the first thing I saw was my husband and our little dog, Angel. He had been reading, and she was keeping him company while I slept. I began to cry. Presence--perhaps the most precious expression of love, and so tragically missing in the neglect experience. In awe of the experience, I was, of course, (gratefully) reminded of the tragedy of its lack.

Attachment

Another brutal police murder of a young Black man, Tyre Nichols, shatters the headlines. Although it is hardly a shock anymore, it is still unbearably shocking: this time, the beating was perpetrated by five cops of his own race. That part is another subject for another day. What struck me, yet again, was how in his final moments, with his final breaths, young Nichols cried out "Mama! Mama!" much as George Floyd had. Attachment is a survival need for us humans, as it is for all mammals. It is what we immediately grasp for and cry for in those moments of agony or terror when survival is at stake. More fundamental than even food, or almost air, its absence is like a slow suffocation. Often we don't even know, or don't know for a long time, like Jennette, just how airless the space is and maybe always has been.

Moments like waking up from anesthesia to a loving presence can bring simple but unutterably profound healing. We can all give that in big and small ways. There are so many reasons why we must wake up to the quiet devastation of neglect.

09

Labyrinth:

Longing, Loss, Leopards

We went to adopt our two little dogs, Button and Angel, in 2009. I had recently begun writing my first book, so I warned my husband that I would not be much of a co-parent for a while. It had been long enough since the second of our two beloved shelties had passed and never one for being dog-less for long, he was willing to sign on as alpha, primary trainer, and chief bottle washer. He began eagerly poring over the rescue sites as I imagine many lonely people do with dating sites. He finally landed on a couple of terrier mutts at a shelter in Sacramento. I remember years ago, a speaker at a conference said, "All terriers have ADD." Being high strung and high energy myself, the quieter, and seemingly monogamous type shelties were the match for me but being the primary caregiver licensed my husband to choose. One wintry Sunday, we piled into his old VW MR2 and set out for Sac.

It was a sweet little shelter, and I remember cruising the various well-kept cages until we found the selected litter. There were about seven of them. Button was a tiny, mostly mushroom-brown puppy with a curly piglet-like tail and expectant, pleading eyes that seemed to say, "Pick me! Pick me!" She reminded me of myself. Although she later grew up to be a mischievous little rascal who would, as the Grateful Dead song said, "steal your face right off your head," we did not know that then. Angel, with a squarish jaw, looked more like a terrier. She had serious, almost sad-looking, wise eyes and scruffy whiskers that reminded me of Einstein. I don't remember the other sibs; I was pretty taken with Button. I was also amazed at how these littermate sisters could look so vastly different.

Button and Angel continued to be inseparable throughout their/our life together. Roommates in the womb, they never had any intention of doing anything different, and indeed they lived up to the ADD prediction. The pups had a good long run together until deep in the pandemic when I was now locked down and home all the time. Button began to have many serious health problems requiring much medical attention, and then twice-a-day fluid infusions. My husband would do the difficult medical part at the back of her ever-skinnier little body, and I would entertain the front end with little scraps of homemade cheese. We did all we could to keep her with us, but her little legs got more and more wobbly, to the point where they would collapse under her. Her heroic and devoted dad diligently carried her up and down the stairs and outside to do her business.

Button finally succumbed in 2020. Admittedly it was somewhat of a relief, as well as being so sad. It had become pretty unbearable for us to watch her suffer, and for Angel as well. When she died, Angel became inconsolable. They had always been together. She could not stop crying. She reminded me of the research I heard of years ago about the blighted twin. When one twin failed to develop and ultimately dissolved away, the other went through life with a deep sense of something being missing. If we ever had to leave her alone, which thankfully during the lockdown year was rare, Angel wailed, like in some of the mourning rituals I remember seeing in movies at school.

Always shy anyway, grief-stricken Angel cleaved to her dad, making a nest at his feet during his long hours in front of the computer.

Finally, after perhaps a year and a half, Angel is finding a regulated, calm state. When her dad goes out, she even has the courage to come upstairs to my home office and, with consent of course, attend a client session. I recently learned that 2015 research showed that human twins in the womb begin reaching toward each other and touching 14 weeks after gestation. The longing for contact begins long before birth.

Loss

Attachment is indeed our most profound and foundational survival need, which is why neglect is the most pervasive and destructive injury of all to humans. Although massively unacknowledged (and I am doing my best to change that!), it quietly wreaks its devastating damage, especially in the realm of relationships. This, of course, has unspeakable ramifications in both individual and collective life. Trauma therapists are well aware that loneliness and interpersonal pain are what drive people, often with deep ambivalence, to our office doors. With neglect, survivors really don't want to need us or our help, but the sense of deadness and isolation, pandemic or not, becomes unlivable.

Recently, I met a charismatic super couple, a physician and an attorney, Laurie was her name the doctor, had recently won a national award in her country. In the past, she might have been someone who intimidated me but she was so approachable and delightful, as was her partner of 36 years. They sat across from me at breakfast; making conversation, I asked if they had children. Like myself, they had long ago opted against it, but somehow ended up telling me the story about the time they accompanied a close friend to China to support her in adopting a baby girl.

When the three roamed the orphanage, not unlike my own experience in Sacramento some 13 years prior, they met up with baby Anna (not her real name.) To the surprised dismay of the prospective adoptive mother, the 18-month-old orphan magnetically reached for Laurie. It was as if she had found the missing part of herself. I remember reading that after nine months of inhabiting the mother's body, living with her rhythms, her voice, her chemistry, the climate of her energetic and emotional vacillations, a baby profoundly knows her. When they are passed, even at birth, to an adoptive parent, they seem to profoundly know, "This is the wrong one!" Little Anna, drawn almost as if by a vacuum aspirator to Laurie, felt as if she had found the right one.

Now in her twenties and recently married, that feeling never changed. Anna's legal mom has had to live with the primary and primal love that her daughter has had and continues to have for Laurie, and secondarily Laurie's wife. Laurie proudly showed me pictures from Anna's wedding not long ago, the two beaming together. Laurie, her wife, and Anna's legal mom have graciously navigated this challenging configuration over now decades. This indescribable, inexplicable, and super-glue-like attachment remains mysterious. What is that?

Leopards

Shortly after that deeply emotional breakfast conversation, I went for a walk through the chilly, idyllic grounds of the quaint New England conference site. The beautiful trees were bare, and it was blessedly quiet. I knew there was a labyrinth on the grounds but did not think much about it, swimming in my feelings about Laurie and Anna. When I stumbled on the labyrinth, I thought perhaps I might try walking it, something I had never thought of doing. I have always said, "You know how they say a leopard can't change its spots? Well, I can!" I change my spots every chance I get. So I entered the maze.

It was an interesting experience; I thought it was like trauma recovery. I felt like I was going around in circles, getting nowhere, hitting dead ends, but if I stayed the course, the path would take me out into the open again. It was remarkable, just like Laurie and Anna have circled, hit dead ends, and kept going, ultimately finding their way out into the open world. Attachment is the ground upon which it is all built: connection, love, and a measure of patience. Anna's adoptive mom heroically gave her a chance and graciously shared the road with Laurie, moving aside to allow space for extended family. What an angel. And with time, all of them, all of us find our way to the opening and out into the world.

10

Fields:

Energy, Transformation, Transcendence

WARNING: *This contains subject matter that may be disturbing to some readers.*

My best friend in kindergarten was Robin Fields. What a great name!

She recently popped into my mind out of absolutely nowhere. Strange how memory is. I don't recall ever thinking of her. Robin was so pretty and feminine, with shiny strawberry blond hair styled in a flip. I loved her mom, Roselyn: she was so American, all the things my family wasn't. She chewed gum, wore tennies, and made those wonderful tuna fish sandwiches on white bread with lots of mayo. She reminded me of Carol Burnett. Best friends are so important to little girls, especially lonely children of neglect. I wonder what happened to Robin. She came to mind when I was thinking about fields.

I have been pondering the vast expanse of energy fields. Admittedly, quantum physics makes my head spin, but I am fascinated by the wordless communication that passes between us energetically and in all sorts of-- what are to me-- mysterious ways. Einstein taught us that everything is made up of particles of energy, which includes the myriad of ways we experience energy in the body. When I first started learning about the brain, I thought mostly in terms of brain chemistry, not electricity or energy transmission, even though that is what firing neurons are. Neurofeedback taught me to start thinking about that.

Now I am learning that everything is energy, including color and music, and emotions and the way they pass between us. Plants communicate with other plants and with animals; we humans communicate with both plants and animals, and with each other, if we are tuned in and aware. What a cacophonous babble of conversation swirls around us at all times. This is not woo woo, although it does seem rather magical. I read about how frequencies and botched/misread transmissions caused disastrous casualties in World War II, but that is for another day.

I know when I sit with clients who have histories of neglect, whose stories are unremembered or not stored in the usual cognitive ways, I must keep all my senses wide open and tuned in for transmissions that may arrive through other media. If I stay mindful of the vibration, the movement, the frequencies in my own body and system: emotions, sensations, images, my own memories, dreams, and songs in my head, I often get quiet, telegraphed messages that inspire me to ask questions that then may reveal new puzzle pieces. Of course, I am scrupulously careful to be receptive and not make up their story! Rather, I ask questions, so the story of absence and missing experiences will find its expression as it can.

I am also struck by how our energetic tone powerfully influences what comes back to us. This certainly is not to cast blame, especially on those with histories of neglect, as our experience is to have no impact.

No matter what we do, nothing comes back, leaving us with a powerful and enduring circuitry of helplessness and futility. This makes for what I have come to call the Three P's of Neglect: passivity, procrastination, and paralysis. Many of us know them all too well.

Something I have been surprised to discover in my own life is that often, when we lead with love, the returns may be surprising. Not always, but enough that it is a worthy practice and an at least aspired to default. It can even make forgiveness fruitful and rewarding sometimes. But that, too, is for another day.

Transformation

One of the perks of my particular brand of insomnia is that I catch late-night BBC broadcasts and often fascinating interviews. I happened to hear an interview with a documentary filmmaker whose 30-minute film Stranger at the Gate was in the running for an Academy Award. I rarely watch movies, being much too stingy with my reading time, but this one compelled me. Inspired, I sent the link to many others.

Richard McKinney, a virtual caricature of the racist, white supremacist hate monger, was a fiercely traumatized Marine Corps war veteran who served many bloody years in combat and participated in numerous horrific atrocities. He joined the Marines as a young man in the futile hope of winning his father's respect. Although he failed in that endeavor, military service successfully removed him from a downhill trajectory of using and selling drugs. McKinney probably would have finished out his sorry days in that bloody world, but injury sent him home to his midwestern state.

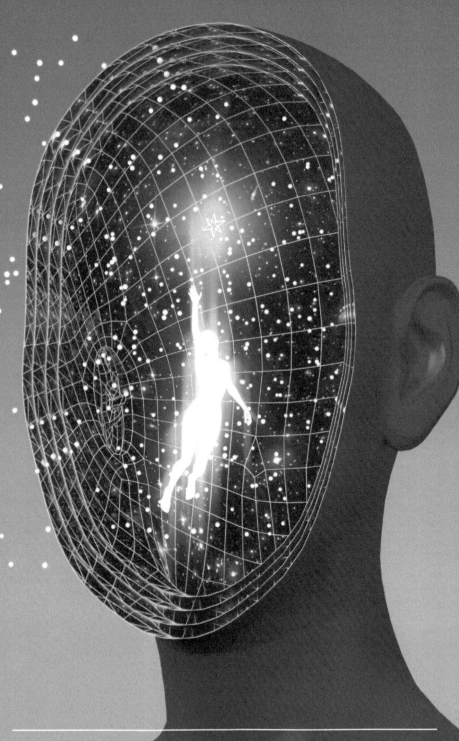

Shortly after his return to the states, 9/11 struck. McKinney, in a blast of PTSD, was inflamed with a wild resurgence of hatred for Muslims. His ordinarily quiet town of Muncie, Indiana, had become a refuge for a sizeable Afghan community with a well-attended mosque. McKinney was seized with the idea of committing mass murder and blowing away as many Muslims as he could, even if it killed him. He began to frequent the mosque, to learn the rhythms of its comings and goings so that he could get the most bang for his buck.

Upon visiting the mosque, McKinney was surprised to be met with such warmth, such welcome, such generosity, such openness, such love, that it first gave him pause, and then transformed him. Not only did McKinney dispense with his catastrophic plan, but his soul opened, and he became a Muslim. It is a must-see, and available for free on YouTube.

Transcendence

So,what does any of this have to do with energy fields? There are so many dimensions of change and transformation. There is such a range of visible and invisible conveyance of development, devastation, decay, healing, and growth. Becoming mindful and intentional, where possible, of what we emit and what we receive/consume can have a powerful impact, though not always. So much trauma of every kind is beyond our control or influence, but there is a sphere of possibility. How could the kind Muslims know that by simply being themselves and practicing their values and beliefs, they were saving themselves from calamity? How can we know? We can't.

My experience teaches me daily that leading with the positive most often brings returns beyond my imagination. In turn, sadly, I observe people who unwittingly, through the pessimistic or resentful energy (or in the grip of depression) they emit, attract a like energetic response. The prophecy is self-fulfilled; they make people not like them, or worse. Not always, of course! But as the Dalai Lama wisely says, "Be kind whenever possible. It is always possible." Although certainly not always easy!

Neurofeedback works directly with brain frequencies, actively training and teaching them to change their tune. We work with frequency in countless ways throughout the day, throughout our respective worlds and the larger world. Tune in! I have often said that one of my most cherished bequests from our mom, starting when I was maybe two in our little slummy apartment in New York City, was Pete Seeger. His upbeat transmissions filled the air, and even though he died in 2014 at the age of 95, in my world, they still do.

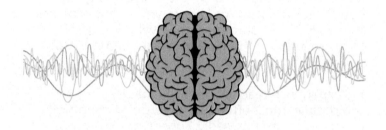

Out of My
Mind

of My

Made in the USA
Columbia, SC
03 May 2023

16067628R00057